Askern Main
& Instoneville

Early Development

Dave Fordham

Published by Fedj-el-Adoum Publishing

3 Adelaide Road, Norton, Doncaster, South Yorkshire, DN6 9EW

© Fedj-el-Adoum Publishing & Dave Fordham 2009

ISBN 978-0-9562864-3-7
First Edition 2009

Cover Illustration:

"Coal Reached at Askern Sep 14th 1912" reads the caption on this postcard by *Regina Press of Doncaster, showing the Union Jack triumphantly flying from the top of the headgear indicating that the No. 1 shaft has located the Barnsley Coal Seam at a depth of 568 yards, after 18 months of sinking operations. The headgears, winding engines and chimney are in place and the colliery appears ready to extract its first coal.*

Askern Main Colliery & Instoneville

Early Development

Askern Colliery in 1914

Acknowledgements

The author would like to thank the following for their assistance in compiling this work:

John Fordham, Joan Ulley & Paul Fox for suggesting improvements to the manuscript; Sid Roe; Terry Goodwin; Colin Bowes; Dennis Ridley; Jennifer Ridley for the notes on her grandfather Herbert Evans; Pete Clements at www.freewebs.com/yorkshiremain for allowing the reproduction of the two photographs by Pat O'Grady; the staff of Doncaster Archives; Helen Wallder and Carol Hill from Doncaster Local Studies Library for allowing access to contemporary newspaper records from *The Doncaster Gazette* and *The Doncaster Chronicle;* the staff of The National Coal Mining Museum for England Library and The University of Birmingham Library for viewing their holdings of *The Colliery Guardian;* and the many picture postcard publishers whose work has been used to illustrate this publication, in particular Edgar Leonard Scrivens and James Simonton & Sons. Unless otherwise attributed, all illustrations featured in this publication are from the author's collection.

A special acknowledgement must be recorded to Margaret Longley who has donated her late husband Stan's Askern photograph albums and notes to BarnSCAN – *The Barnsdale Local History Group.* Stan Longley worked for many years at Askern Coalite and following his retirement he dedicated the rest of his life to researching all aspects of the history of Askern and was a great inspiration to the author.

Askern Main Colliery

During the 19th Century, Askern was locally famous for its lake and spa and had become a fashionable watering place. People would visit from all over the country to take the waters in the town's 5 spa houses. However, changes were afoot during the early 1900s when the local landowners of the district began to negotiate leases for the coal which was believed to underlie their estates and a new colliery was proposed. This came as a shock to the villagers of Askern, especially when the site of the new pit was later moved to the hill overlooking the village in an attempt to cut costs. However, it would take several years for the new colliery to reach its full potential following developmental difficulties and several changes in ownership.

E.L.S. 24-2. THE SPA AND HYDRO, ASKERN.

Askern as pictured on a postcard published by Edgar Scrivens around 1907. At the beginning of the 20th century, Askern was a modest spa town with five public bath houses surrounding Askern Lake together with substantial villas where people taking the waters could obtain lodgings. The Spa Hydropathic Establishment is the large building at the rear centre overlooking the lake. The "Spa Hydro" would later become the first Miners Welfare and would itself be overshadowed by the Colliery and Coalite works which were built on the skyline overlooking the village of Askern.

The first organisation with an interest in the Askern area was The Don Coal & Iron Co. Ltd. which was registered with a capital of £150,000 in 1903 with the aim of securing coal leases and developing a number of collieries. The initial subscribers to the capital included the following:

H A Allport, Dodworth Grove, Barnsley, (Chairman)
E A Allport, Lound House, Haxey
D J Williams, Barnsley
W R Percy, Nottingham
Plus 3 London solicitors.

They were later joined by Wilfred Tempest of Ackworth Hall, and the newly formed company began negotiating the leases for the coal beneath a large area in the River Went Valley between Pontefract and Doncaster. This included the coal lying under Wilfred Tempest's own estate at Ackworth and that from the Bacon-Franks of Campsall Hall, the Cooke-Yarboroughs of Campsmount and the Davis-Cookes of Owston Hall. In the autumn of 1903, The Don Coal & Iron Co. announced ambitious plans for the development of four collieries at Ackworth, Darrington, Kirk Smeaton and Askern.

Negotiations continued with the landowners in 1904, and in July 1905 The Don Coal & Iron Co. proposed to build their own railway line from Ackworth to Shaftholme Junction near Bentley which Wilfred Tempest thought would service the four collieries alongside the line that the company proposed to develop. The sinking of the first pit at Askern was expected to cost £200,000 and by the time the other three pits were developed the company intended to employ 6,000 men in total.

By 1906 the site of the new Askern Colliery had been chosen on land belonging to Mr Davis-Cooke of Owston Hall at Shaftholme, adjacent to the company's proposed railway line. However, the Don Coal & Iron Co. was experiencing problems in raising the finance for its ambitious plan for four collieries and the associated railway line. In an attempt to reduce costs the site for Askern Colliery was moved from Shaftholme to the hill top overlooking the Spa Hydro and Askern Lake, because there was a nearby connection with the Lancashire & Yorkshire Railway's Knottingley branch line that ran through Askern village. By 1909 the projected cost of the new Askern Colliery had escalated to £400,000, double that which was quoted only four years ago. Preparations for sinking started during 1909 when the proposed site was levelled but the Don Iron and Coal Co. was still having trouble raising the £400,000 capital required and the project looked increasingly likely to be stillborn.

The coal seams beneath the Askern area were leased from the estates of the Bacon-Frank family of Campsall Hall and the Cooke-Yarborough family of Campsmount. Both residences were situated in the village of Campsall to the west of Askern. The Bacon-Frank family left Campsall Hall in 1942 as allegedly Mrs Bacon-Frank believed the estate had been spoilt by the proximity of Askern Colliery. Campsall Hall survived as flats until demolition in 1986. The Cooke-Yarborough family sold Campsmount in 1935 to the West Riding County Council and the building was demolished in the 1950s. (Postcards Published by Edgar Leonard Scrivens).

7

However in March 1910 things were looking up when the Blaina Coal & Iron Company from Monmouthshire and the Bestwood Coal & Iron Company from Nottinghamshire announced that they had formed a joint consortium to acquire the proposed Askern Colliery from The Don Coal & Iron Co. The new owners registered The Askern Coal and Iron Company Ltd. of 55 High Street, Doncaster, with a capital of £400,000 to "purchase, take lease or otherwise acquire any collieries or coal mines and iron and other mines and to carry on the business of colliery proprietors and iron masters". The Signatories and first directors of the new company included:

John Lancaster, Dunchurch Lodge, Rugby
James Lancaster, The Woodlands, Blaina, Monmouthshire
G W Lancaster, St George's House, Eastcheap, London
M Wolstenholme, Stanfoist House, Abergevenny
H T Bailey, 4 St Dunstan's Alley, London
R Gardner, Maisemore, Abergevenny

The Lancaster family owned the Blania Coal & Iron Co. and they quickly took control of the new company, installing Mr Llewellyn-Jones as manager and the erstwhile Don Coal & Iron Co. was wound up. In addition to the 7,391 acres of coal lease that had been secured by the previous owners from the Campsmount, Campsall & Owston Hall estates, the new company began to negotiate for a further 8,000 acres from small proprietors in the neighbourhood. The plan was to secure a huge royalty lying beneath the land between the Great North Road near Wentbridge in the west and the New Junction Canal near Sykehouse in the east. Before the shafts would be developed it was announced that a trial borehole would be sunk. The new owners had privately raised £500,000 without appealing to the public and they believed this would be sufficient capital to develop the colliery and its adjacent housing estate. In 1910, £500,000 was a considerable sum of money to outlay before a single lump of coal could be sold.

Things started to proceed in the autumn of 1910 when the contract for sinking the colliery was given to Messrs Charles Walker & Co. who had successfully completed the sinking of Hickleton and Bentley Collieries and around 300-400 pit sinkers moved on to the site. The pit sinkers were the navvies of their day and moved from colliery to colliery to undertake the highly specialised and dangerous work of excavating the shafts. They were accommodated in temporary wooden huts near Campsall Road. Preparations were made for constructing a short railway line over Campsall Road to connect the pit with the nearby Lancashire & Yorkshire Railway. Over the forthcoming winter with the railway line and bridge in place, equipment was transported to the site and the contractors commenced the construction of the surface buildings. The trial borehole was put down on the site of the No. 1 shaft to prove the existence of the coal seams within the underlying coal measures rocks.

Postcard from around 1911 entitled "Making The Colliery Askern". Material around the site was moved by the steam powered cranes. An ancillary building is nearing completion and the pile of bricks for constructing the engine house would have been brought in from the nearby brickworks located to the north of Campsall Road (Postcard by Regina Press, Stan Longley Collection).

On February 22nd 1911, the directors held a small ceremony to mark the cutting of the first sod at their new Askern Colliery. Judging by the experiences at nearby Bentley and Bullcroft Collieries, they expected to encounter a large volume of water during the sinking of the two 21.5 feet diameter shafts. The newly appointed general manager, Mr Llewellyn-Jones, announced that the sinking operations were expected to last two years and it was hoped to discover the Barnsley Coal Seam at a depth of around 700 yards. The new venture was expected to employ 4,000 men who would produce 1,000,000 tons of coal per year. Additional men would be required as the company intended to also build an iron and steel works adjacent to the pit. The trial borehole had been abandoned in the coal measures rocks at a depth of 375 yards because the promoters had by now gained enough confidence that the Barnsley Coal Seam would be found, judging by the results at nearby Brodsworth, Bentley and

9

Bullcroft Collieries. As the royalty was largely beneath agricultural land it was hoped to extract all the coal apart from that lying beneath Askern village which would be left intact to prevent the effects of subsidence. Mr Llewellyn-Jones also announced the construction of a model village of 1,000 houses adjacent to Sutton Road to house the workforce.

Askern Brickworks in 1911 as depicted on a postcard by Regina Press of Doncaster. Two large kilns are under construction together with the base of the brickworks chimney which would eventually become one of the tallest chimneys in Yorkshire. The brickworks (shown as Askern Brick and Tile Works on the map on Page 24) were located to the north of the colliery and ceased production in the 1960s when the site was covered by an extension to the colliery spoil heap. The clay pits which supplied the works were to the west of the colliery (shown as Askern Field on the map) and have been landscaped as part of Campsall Country Park).

In the following weeks, perhaps in recognition that Askern's days as a health resort would soon be over, the owners of the Askern Spa Hydropathic establishment sold the building to the Sheffield Breweries who intended to convert the Hydro into a social club and institute for the incoming miners. The remaining public spa buildings, the South Parade Baths, Terrace Baths, Charity Baths and Manor Baths closed down in the 1920s and 1930s due to dwindling visitor numbers and all five bath houses had been demolished by the 1960s.

Construction of No. 2 engine house viewed from Campsall Road in early 1911. Both engine houses were provided with a 1911 date stone positioned in the gable end facing the shafts. The purpose of the row of small chimneys on the left is unknown; they were possibly used as temporary steam raising boilers. Whatever, they would soon be dismantled and replaced with the screens and coal preparation plant. (Postcard by Regina Press).

By April 1911, the shafts were 40 yards deep when the new venture suffered its first setback. Overnight the shafts had filled up with water from the springs that fed Askern Lake and the villagers were surprised to awake one day to discover that Askern Lake had drained dry, causing waterfront properties to subside. It was announced that the shafts would be lined with iron tubbing to stop the flow of water into the shafts which would enable Askern Lake to fill with water and this eventually occurred by the spring of 1912. In the meantime the colliery company, with an eye to making some revenue, pumped the water out of the shafts and sold it to the Doncaster Rural Council water supply.

By the summer of 1912, the surface buildings had been completed and the erection of steel lattice headgears above No. 1 and No. 2 shafts was under hand. The winding engines were in place and the pit would be able to produce coal as soon as the Barnsley Coal Seam was reached. No. 1 shaft was now over 300 yards deep but No. 2 was only 90 yards deep as this had been started later on December 5th 1911. No. 1 shaft was intended to reach coal by Christmas 1912.

*Askern Colliery Developments in early 1911 as featured on postcards published by Regina Press of Doncaster. **Above:** Building the railway bridge over Campsall Road enabling the pit site to be connected with the nearby Lancashire & Yorkshire Railway. **Below:** Constructing surface buildings. The wagons belong to Charles Baker & Sons, Railway Contractors of Chesterfield who were employed to build the railway and sidings. (Both Stan Longley Collection).*

As it was, the shaft sinking proceeded far more fortuitously than had been expected and the directors were proud to announce that the No. 1 shaft had found the Barnsley Coal Seam on Saturday 14th September 1912, at a depth of 568 yards, well short of the expected depth of 700 yards. It had only taken 18 months to sink the No. 1 shaft to a depth of 568 yards which was believed to be a record at the time. Very few difficulties had been experienced during the sinking, apart from the leak of 4,000 gallons per minute when Askern Lake was drained in April 1911. The Barnsley Coal Seam was a good nine feet thick, but in this area of the Yorkshire Coalfield the Barnsley seam had split into two levels separated by three yards of shale. The upper level was named the Warren House Seam and it was this seam that would be mined first. The whole of the surface plant was ready to extract coal from a coalfield of 15,000 acres. It was intended that No. 1 shaft would work the Barnsley (Warren House) Seam and that No. 2 shaft would be extended down to a greater depth to exploit the Dunsil, Haigh Moor and Flockton Seams.

Another postcard published in early 1912 by Regina Press whose photographs of the development of Askern Colliery appeared in The Doncaster Gazette on a regular basis. Both engine houses and the connecting power house with adjacent chimney have been completed together with a stores building on the left. Construction of the steel lattice headgear above No. 1 shaft is underway, although one leg of the frame and the winding wheels have yet to be hoisted in to position.

This postcard view by Edgar Scrivens of c1914 is taken from Campsall Road. Two steel lattice headgears of No. 2 shaft (left) and No. 1 shaft (right) are situated behind corresponding winding engine houses linked by a power house behind the large chimney. The buildings look well constructed and appear ready to handle coal production. At the time the two winding engine houses were equipped with the largest colliery steam winding engines in the country.

On January 10th 1913, the No. 2 shaft finally encountered the Barnsley Coal Seam but the colliery company was disappointed to find that the coal had been disturbed by geological faults. This would require additional expenditure and a sloping tunnel or drift at the bottom of the shaft would have to be constructed to connect the various levels of coal seams. The shafts were continued downwards to access the Flockton Coal Seam at a depth of 720 yards. However, the faulting of the coal seams around the base of the shaft and the resultant hindering of coal extraction would ultimately lead to the downfall of The Askern Coal & Iron Company.

During the war years 1914-1918, slow progress was made with developing the underground roadways from the base of the shafts in order to access the undisturbed areas of the coal seams. The Warren House Seam was opened out and the colliery went in to small scale production but was far from reaching its full potential. Nevertheless, by 1918 production had achieved its highest rate to date at 6,704 tons per week and 952 men were employed but this was still not a high enough figure to enable a profit to be made.

By 1918, six years after first encountering the Barnsley Coal Seam, the Askern Coal & Iron Co. was on the verge of bankruptcy as since 1909, the Lancaster family had invested around £600,000 in developing the pit and building a model village for the workforce, but had not yet seen any return on their money as the geological faulting of the coal seams was hampering production. This must have been very frustrating for the directors, as the neighbouring pits of Brodsworth, Bentley and Bullcroft were by now in full production and making good profits for their owners. It was no surprise when, at the end of 1918, Askern Colliery underwent its third change in ownership with the appearance of the charismatic Welshman, Samuel "Sammy" Instone.

Samuel Instone was born in Gravesend, Kent in 1879 but moved to Cardiff in 1899 where he gained employment as a shipping manager for a shipping company with offices in Cardiff. In 1908 he went into business with his brothers Theodore and Alfred as coal merchants and they formed S. Instone & Co. Ltd. and commenced distributing coal from the South Wales collieries. In 1914 they bought their first ship named *Collivaud* and by 1918 they had a fleet of twelve steamers exporting coal from Cardiff docks. They also provided one of the first cross channel passenger ferry services. The war years had proved to be very profitable and the Instone Brothers were keen to purchase their own colliery with the intention of supplying their own fleet of ships with a cheap source of coal. When they heard that the Askern Coal & Iron Co. was in financial trouble they acquired the controlling interest in December 1918.

As well as owning a fleet of ships, in 1919 the Instone brothers formed the pioneering Instone Airline flying from the UK to France and other European destinations. However, in 1924 Instone Air was sold to Imperial Airways following Government reorganisation of the airline industry. At the time of publication Instone Air is still in business as a speciality freight carrier.

Returning to 1919 and the Instone Brothers travelled to Askern to announce their ambitious plans for the area. The Askern Coal & Iron Co. Ltd. had become a wholly owned subsidiary of S. Instone & Co. Ltd. with Samuel Instone as the new Chairman and his brother Theodore as Managing Director. The property had been valued at £771,944 and had an estimated 496,000,000 tons of coal within its royalty. The brothers announced that they would develop the pit so that it would be capable of handling 4,000 tons of coal per day or 30,000 tons per week. Perhaps with delusions of grandeur, they proudly predicted that the pit would produce 1,000,000 tons of coal per year for the next 134 years from the Barnsley, Warren House and Flockton Coal Seams. When these seams would be exhausted in the year 2054, the mining of other coal seams would sustain the output for a further 300 years. With the benefit of hindsight, their proposals appear some what exaggerated!

In 1919, the Instone Brothers registered a new company, The Askern Coke & By-Products Syndicate Ltd, to develop a coking works next to the pit at a cost of £400,000. This would later become the Doncaster Coalite Works. The brothers also established The Askern Garden City Utility Association whose aim was to build 700 houses which would surround the model village which had been built by the previous owners. They intended to press Doncaster Corporation to construct a public tramway system to connect Askern with Doncaster. In 1920 they re-named the model village "Instoneville" and the colliery wagons that they had inherited were repainted with S. Instone & Co. lettering on their sides.

In 1921 when Samuel Instone was knighted, he went on another buying spree when he purchased the Bedwas Navigation Colliery at Newport, South Wales for £508,000. The two pits Askern and Bedwas would supply the firm's ships with coal. In 1924 another pit, The Hoyland Silkstone Colliery near Barnsley was bought but this was sold on after only a year when S. Instone & Co. decided to focus their resources on Askern and Bedwas.

At the beginning of 1920, Askern Colliery employed 1,200 men who produced around 5,000 tons of coal per week. A start was made at tapping the Barnsley Seam beneath the Warren House Seam and in the early 1920s roadways and coalfaces were opened out in the Smeaton and Pollington districts of the mine. As the decade progressed the output slowly increased and in 1923 a Simon Carves Ltd. "Baum" washery was opened to process the coal and extensive coal screens were constructed over the railway sidings where the coal could be loaded directly into trains of wagons. Waste spoil was transported to the tip on the other side of Campsall Road by a pair of aerial ropeways. At the end of 1923 output had reached 7,000 tons per week and 1,643 men were employed.

By the end of 1925 the pit was now producing 9,000 tons of coal per week and the workforce had increased to 1,956. Unfortunately for Sir Samuel Instone, the colliery was still not making a profit as although output was increasing the price of coal was beginning to fall. The company was being sustained with profits from its shipping interests. The General Strike of 1926 saw scenes of hardship at Askern, with conflicts between the workers and the management who were keen to get the men back to work in order to increase production. Things became particularly heated between Sir Samuel Instone and Herbert Smith, the president of the Miners Federation of Great Britain Union. In a dispute which reached the courts Herbert Smith called Sir Samuel Instone "a welsh swindler" and "Sammy

E.L.S. 27-73. Askern Main Colliery

Two postcard views captured by Edgar Scrivens from the public right of way connecting Instoneville to Askern Village, carried by a long foot bridge over the railway sidings. The views were photographed 10 years apart, dated 1914 and 1924 respectively and illustrate some of the developments undertaken by S. Instone & Co. Ltd. These include the enclosing of the upcast No. 2 shaft with a reinforced concrete collar to aid ventilation and the completion of the coal washery and coal preparation plant, work undertaken by Plowright Engineering of Chesterfield. The spare winding wheel lying horizontally in the foreground remains in both pictures.

27-36. Askern Main Colliery.

of the black hearts" but he was then sued by Sir Samuel Instone who was successfully awarded damages for slander.

In the last years of the 1920s production at Askern Colliery began to rise again and by the end of the decade production reached 10,000 tons per week. The workforce had increased to 2,835 men and the colliery was finally in profit for the first time.

In 1928 S. Instone & Co. Ltd. formed a partnership with Low Temperature Carbonisation Ltd. to form Doncaster Coalite Ltd. It was proposed to build a large coking plant on a site adjacent to Askern Colliery and the coke works would produce "*Coalite*" coke directly from Askern coal. Other by-products would be produced by the distillation of coal and weekly production of the following was announced:

Coalite Coke, 3,000 tons
Crude Oil, 28,000 gallons
Motor Spirit, 3,000 gallons
Gas, 6,500,000 cubic feet.
Ammonia and Ammonium Sulphate, 12 tons.

150 men would be employed at the coke works and gas and electricity would be supplied to the villages of Askern, Campsall, Norton and Sutton. For the next 60 years the distinctive smell of coke production would hang over Askern village.

Askern Coalite was formerly opened by Miss Ellen Wilkinson M.P. on July 5th 1929, when she switched on the motor operating the tippler for the first batch of coal. However the coking plant soon ran into controversy when in October of 1929 complaints about the new works were read out at an Askern Parish Council meeting. The Selby Road School Headmaster said "can not anything be done to prevent the Coalite people from flooding the village with their filthy disgusting gas?" as he claimed it was effecting the health of his pupils and teachers who were suffering from vomiting, headache and diarrhoea. The Askern Church vicar said he had received many complaints from villagers. The Parish Council referred the matter to Doncaster Rural District Council whose medical officer visited the plant and the emissions were brought under control.

On 31st May 1930 whilst opening the new Miners Welfare Park at Askern, Sir Samuel Instone gave a speech. He said that he firmly believed that at Askern they had reached a turning point and that all their efforts were going to be fruitful at last. The Coalite plant had been a tremendous success and was already in profit and the pit was at last moving into profit. The following year S. Instone & Co. Ltd. announced that they had recorded a profit of £7,121 for the year 1930, mostly from the shipping division and their stake in Doncaster Coalite. The capital of the Company was valued at £871,942.

In 1930 with the onset of the Great Depression the Mines Act (1930) saw the introduction of the Quota System imposed by the Government on the various colliery companies. To avoid a glut in over production with the consequent collapse in the price of coal, each colliery was given a fixed tonnage of coal to produce. When that figure had been reached the pit would have to close for the rest of the year until they received the following year's quota. This news was particularly disappointing for the directors of S. Instone & Co. as the colliery had only just moved into profit after ten years of investment and they had hoped to increase production. In 1932 the manger of the colliery, Mr Llewellyn-Jones, who had now been in this position for 21 years, stated that due to the tonnage quota, Askern was only producing 12,000 tons per week, rather than 18,500 and was therefore operating at 66% of capacity. He had hoped to raise 825,000 tons of coal in 1932 but due to the quota system they were only allowed to produce 500,000 tons which had now been achieved and he had to dismiss 700 miners as there was no work for them.

The unstable economic conditions continued throughout the 1930s with increasing annoyance to the mine owners. By 1935, the pit was capable of producing 1,200,000 tons but this was capped back by the quota system, which was stifling the potential for profit from the colliery. The quota system remained in place until the outbreak of World War II, when production was increased to meet the country's war requirements. By this time Askern Colliery was at last contributing towards making a profit for its owners but unfortunately for Sir Samuel Instone he never lived to see the pit produce the large profit that he had anticipated as he died in 1937. During the war years, S. Instone & Co. Ltd. recorded the following profits:

1940: £32,265
1941: £46,817
1942: £39,661
1943: £44,835

However coal production was still not as high as it could have been due to a staff shortage as many of the men had left to join the army even though mining was a protected occupation. The shortage of workers was partially solved by the introduction of Bevin Boys.

Aerial view of the Askern Coalite Plant looking south east in the 1960s. Askern Market Place is top left and Instoneville is on the upper right hand side. Askern Colliery is off camera to the left from which coal was transported by the conveyor to the large bunker in the centre for grading prior to being fed into the row of 18 coking ovens or batteries where the coal was transformed into the smokeless fuel "Coalite". The production of Coalite was patented in 1906 by Thomas Parker who established British Coalite Ltd. who operated two small plants at Plymouth and Barking. British Coalite was restructured in 1917 as Low Temperature Carbonisation Ltd., following the takeover of The Barnsley Smokeless Fuel Company. Plants were established at Barugh near Barnsley (1917), Askern (1928), East Greenwich (1929), Bolsover (1936), Wern Tarw in South Wales (1939), Grimethorpe (1966), & Rossington (1972). The Askern operation was operated jointly with S. Instone & Co. under the trading name 'Doncaster Coalite' and generated significant profits for S. Instone & Co., probably a greater percentage than those produced by Askern Colliery. The Askern Coalite Plant was decommissioned in 1986 and was subsequently demolished in 1987/8. (Photographer unknown, Stan Longley Collection)

On the 1st January 1947, the mines were nationalised, much to the pleasure of the employees, and the National Coal Board (N.C.B.) took over the management of Askern Colliery from S. Instone & Co. Theodore and Alfred Instone and the other directors were financially compensated and they retired from the business. At this time coal production at Askern Colliery had fallen to 409,000 tons in 1947 with 2,465 employed. During the 1950s output increased as the number employed decreased due to the advances in mechanisation and 700,000 tons were produced in 1958. The colliery was fully modernised both underground and on the surface which included the erection of pithead baths and new winding gear for No. 2 shaft with skip winding facilities. The N.C.B. also built the white-cladded coal preparation plant which, together with the water tower, headgears and the Coalite plant, came to form a distinctive skyline over the village of Askern. Alongside the coal preparation plant was a newly constructed rapid loading bunker. Here large amounts of coal were loaded on to "merry go round" trains which took the coal directly to the Aire Valley power stations. From the coal preparation plant, a conveyor carried spoil across Campsall Road and on to the tip and the aerial ropeways were dismantled. The spoil tip grew larger and larger and progressively covered more fields towards the Norton direction, burying part of Norton Common Lane in the process.

During the 1950s and 1960s smaller collieries in the Scotland and Northumberland areas which had exhausted their coal reserves were being closed by the N.C.B. whilst the Doncaster coalfield was about to enter another boom period. Consequently miners were transferred to the Doncaster area and additional housing was built by the N.C.B. and the Local Authority in Askern and Campsall to house these incoming miners. Production at Askern Colliery finally peaked at 750,000 tons in 1975, well short of the claims made by Sir Samuel Instone back in 1919. Unlike many of the other collieries on the Doncaster coalfield, Askern Colliery never managed to break the 1,000,000 tons of coal per year barrier.

After the Miners' Strike of 1984/5, the Coalite Plant was closed and subsequently demolished removing it from the Askern skyline. British Coal, as the N.C.B. had now been renamed, earmarked the pit for closure and most men worked their final shift in December 1991. The last coal left by train on Friday 13th March 1992 and the distinctive smell from the Coalite Plant that used to hang in the air over Askern is now a memory.

All the colliery buildings were demolished during 1993 and the two shafts were capped with methane extractors to allow mine gases to escape from the abandoned workings. The long footbridge over the former railway sidings carrying the footpath from Instoneville to Askern remained in place until 1999 when the derelict site underwent transformation into Warren House Park. The spoil tip passed in to the ownership of UK Coal following the privatisation of British Coal in 1994 and for the next few years the tip was used for the dumping of truck loads of colliery spoil from UK Coal's Kellingley Colliery. The spoil tip was finally landscaped in 2000. At the time of writing the spoil heap has not been transformed into an amenity area like many of the neighbouring slag heaps. In 2009 from the top of Askern spoil tip the headgears of four surviving collieries are visible at Kellingley, Hatfield, Harworth and Maltby.

Askern Colliery dominated the village for over 80 years, and the future for Askern now perhaps lies as a commuter village for people who work in Doncaster and Leeds. Maybe Askern will return to its original form as a spa town and leisure resort focused around Askern Lake? The pit winding wheels have been positioned at the Miners Welfare and at Alexander House as a memorial to all those who worked at Askern Colliery.

The Askern skyline in the 1980s, viewed from the road between Campsall & Sutton villages. The colliery is on the left where the original winding engine house and headgear for No. 2 shaft can be seen. A new headgear and winding engine house has been provided for No. 1 shaft by the N.C.B.'s modernisation programme. The white buildings in the centre are the N.C.B. built coal preparation plant and rapid loading bunker. To the right behind the houses of Instoneville is the large grey Coalite bunker; behind are the black coloured buildings consisting of a battery of 18 coking ovens which partially obscure the water tower. Later housing from the 1950s is visible at the top end of Instoneville. (Photo by Pat O'Grady, courtesy of www.freewebs.com/yorkshiremain).

Instoneville

Whilst the two shafts were being sunk to the Barnsley Coal Seam in 1911, preparations were also under way to construct a model village to house the workforce. This was in the days before the provision of council housing by local authorities and one of the methods by which a colliery owner could recruit and retain a workforce was by providing a company-owned house for the miner and his family. This could become a profitable enterprise as the rent for the house would be deducted from the miner's wages and this rent would then be a guaranteed income. In the event that the miners went on strike they were liable for eviction from their company-owned house which could then be used to accommodate non-striking miners.

The owners of Askern Colliery commissioned Doncaster's Regina Press Photographers to record the construction process at the pit and several of Regina's postcards are used to illustrate this work including this example depicting the steam powered navvy, an excavator at work clearing the site for the new village of Instoneville. The spoil was loaded into wagons which were taken away and tipped to form the embankment of the branch line connecting the site to the Lancashire & Yorkshire Railway.

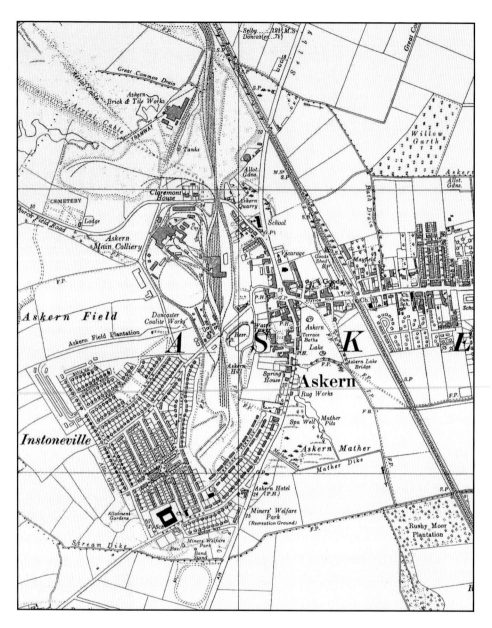

Extract from the 1955 Ordnance Survey 6" to the mile map of the Askern area featuring some of the locations mentioned in the text. The colliery complex with the associated railway sidings and Doncaster Coalite Works separates the new village of Instoneville in the east, built to house the workforce, from the old village of Askern in the west clustered around Askern Lake and the Railway Station. Extending from the colliery are two aerial cables or ropeways where waste material was tipped onto the fields of the Norton Common area. (Crown Copyright reserved).

A site for the new village had been located between the colliery and Sutton Road on the ridge of land overlooking the old village of Askern. However, the land required levelling and grading and the contractors brought in a large steam powered excavator to clear the site. This remarkable rail mounted machine featured in the newspapers of the day and must have been looked on in awe by the residents of the old village as it excavated the soil like a steam powered mechanical dinosaur! By the end of 1911, the work of this excavator, known as the 'Puffing Billy' had been completed and the site had been levelled into a steady gradient leading down to Sutton Road and construction of the housing commenced. A small railway line was extended from the colliery along Green Lane, The Avenue and Victoria Road to transport building materials to the site.

The bricks for the new village would be sourced locally from two brickworks, one near Moss Station and the other much nearer to the colliery. The Askern Brickworks were established by The Hardy Brick & Tile Co. who constructed several brick ovens and a very tall chimney. Clay was transported from the clay pits near Campsall Hall to the Askern Brickworks which were located on a site between the Campsall and Selby Roads.

The Askern Coal & Iron Co. established the Askern Estates Co. Ltd. in 1911 with a budget of £5,000 to build the new village. The first directors of Askern Estates included Mr Humble, a manager from the pit, and Mr Leadley of Goldthorpe near Barnsley, a house builder who had constructed most of the housing in Goldthorpe for the Hickleton Main Colliery Co. Mr Leadley was awarded the contract for the construction of the proposed 2,366 houses. 1,500 of these would be built on the Sutton Road site whilst 866 would be constructed on a second site adjacent to Moss Road, a proposal that was later abandoned. Mr Humble stated that the housing would be built at a density of 20 per acre and he said that no buildings would be seen in Askern Model Village like some of those built at Carcroft which he claimed were a disgrace to civilisation. The first houses to be built were a pair of large villas for managers, including Claremount House, situated opposite the colliery gates on Campsall Road.

The first years of the 20th Century saw the introduction of a more enlightened attitude towards the construction of workers' housing following the dreary terraces in industrial areas of the Victorian period. This had culminated locally with the opening of Woodlands Model Village by the Brodsworth Main Colliery Co. in 1907/8. However, Askern Model Village was laid out in an uninspiring grid pattern of parallel streets which were orientated perpendicularly to Sutton Road. No attempt was made to imitate the garden suburb layout of Woodlands with its curved avenues and green open spaces, although there were some attempts to limit the worst features of speculative development, where in other colliery areas private builders had built poor quality housing and rented these directly to the miners. Despite the Askern Colliery Company officially referring to the new housing as 'Askern Model Village' it became known as New Village by the residents. The houses were provided with three small bedrooms upstairs although there was no provision for a bathroom as the men usually bathed in a tin bath in the downstairs scullery or front room.

By 1912, Park Road, Manor Road, and The Avenue had been constructed at right angles to Sutton Road and the three streets were connected by Victoria Road which ran parallel to Sutton Road. Houses were built in blocks of varying number, mostly in groups of 5, 6 or 8, although some of the terraces were 12 and 13 houses long. However, while 1,500 houses were originally planned for this site, the Askern Estates Co had only constructed 247 houses plus six shops on Sutton Road and the two villas for managers on Campsall Road, a total of 255 houses, when building work came to a halt at the end of 1913. This was because of the financial expenditure that was being incurred at the colliery in opening out the coal reserves due to the faulted nature of the rocks below ground.

In the meantime an area of land had been set aside for the West Riding County Council who opened a tin school in 1913 to serve the children of the New Village on Sutton Road. The tin school was eventually replaced with a more substantial brick built school. Provision had been made for various shops on Victoria and Sutton Roads and it was proposed that Askern Model Village would exist as an independent community without the need for the inhabitants to shop in the old village of Askern.

As well as local people, workers came from all over the country to work in the pit, especially from the older coal mining areas of the West Midlands, Northumberland, Wales and Scotland such that Askern became a place of numerous accents. With the opening of the new colliery, the population of Askern rapidly increased from 988 in 1911 to 5,689 in 1921. There was immense pressure for housing from this rapid influx of population in the years up to 1914 as many people regarded the opening of the colliery as a guaranteed job for life. Consequently there was a waiting list for houses in the Model Village. Askern's Victorian villas and guest houses in the old village which had previously housed visitors to Askern Spa now let their rooms to incoming miners and their families. Many of the early miners that came from outside the area had left their family at home whilst they took lodgings in the old village of Askern until they were able to secure a company house whereupon they sent for their own family to join them.

Two postcard views from c1914. **Above:** Victoria Road photographed by Edgar Scrivens and captioned "Model Village", the term used by the colliery company. Edwin Thorpe's off licence was located on the corner with Manor Road. **Below:** Manor Road photographer by Walter Roelich and captioned "New Village", the term used by the residents. The houses were arranged along straight rows in a grid pattern.

The struggle to obtain housing is illustrated by the case of the Evans family. In 1913, Herbert Evans left Burslem in Staffordshire where the pit at which he was employed at was on short time. Herbert and several other men managed to obtain lodgings in the old village of Askern and he reported to Askern Colliery for work. After completing a probationary period he was able to go on the waiting list for a company-owned house. Every day he would queue up at the colliery offices to see if a house had become available. One day in 1914, he joined the queue at the offices and the men in front of him were told there were no houses but when Herbert enquired he was told that a house had been allocated to him and his family at 43 Victoria Road but only on the condition that he would take in two lodgers who like him were also colliery workers. Herbert Evans always put down the reason that he was allocated a house was that he had reported to the office every day in a collar and tie whereas the other men in the queue wore mufflers! The rest of his family, his wife Jane and their children; a son also called Herbert, and two daughters Winnie and Norah, travelled from Staffordshire by train to start their new life in Askern. Jane Herbert always said that she was happy to find that Askern was surrounded by green and pleasant countryside after her upbringing in the smoky potteries of Staffordshire.

Due to the pressure for accommodation many local builders undertook the building of speculative private houses which could be rented privately by miners often at a higher rate than the colliery houses which were in short supply as Herbert Evans had discovered. Several terraces were built in the Norton area by speculative builders as early as 1910 when the colliery site was not yet fixed. Other houses were built by speculative builders on Kings Road and Queens Road in the Moss Road area of Askern and on completion they were soon let to miners and their families.

Between 1910 and the outbreak of the First World War, the old village centre of Askern developed almost into a small town to serve the rapidly expanding population. Many of the old stone built cottages along High Street and Station Road were demolished and replaced with rows of brick built shops which included a new post office and a branch of The Doncaster Mutual Co-operative Society. In 1920 Askern Picture House opened and this became a popular centre of entertainment. The square in front of The Swan Hotel, previously used as a meeting place for the Badsworth Hunt, became a small market place.

Some visitors still came to Askern to sample the waters but in ever decreasing numbers and by the 1960s the remaining bath houses; the Terrace Baths, Manor Baths, Charity Baths and South Parade Baths had been demolished. A fifth bath house, the Spa Hydropathic Establishment had housed the Miners Welfare

Institute since 1924 but due to structural problems this building was declared unsafe in the 1960s and was subsequently demolished and the Miners Welfare Institute moved to purpose built premises on Alfred Road. In the 1920s, Askern Lake became the centre of a park and pleasure grounds with band performances taking place on one of the islands and the hiring of rowing boats became a popular pastime for many Askern folk.

Returning to the new village, the outbreak of World War I and the financial expenditure at the colliery had put a stop to any further building and during the war years many of the houses suffered from overcrowding, with sometimes two or three families sharing a house. In 1918 the Askern Coal & Iron Co Ltd was acquired by S. Instone & Co. Ltd. The new owners, recognising the dire need for more housing, established The Askern Garden City Utility Association which was charged with the construction of further housing. One of the first things the new owners did was to change the name for the colliery housing estate from Askern Model Village to Instoneville in honour of their chairman Samuel Instone and the shops on Sutton Road were renamed Instone Villas.

The Askern Hotel and Sutton Road as depicted on a postcard by Arjay Productions published in the 1950s. The housing on this part of Sutton Road, built in the 1920s by S. Instone's Askern Garden City Utility Association, was much more spacious than the housing provided 10 years earlier by the previous owners of the colliery. The Askern Hotel was built in 1923 by Mappin's Old Masborough Brewery of Rotherham.

In 1920 the first of 176 houses were constructed in blocks of 4 along The Avenue, Sutton Road, Instone Terrace and Doncaster Road. Each of these three bed-roomed houses was supplied with a small front garden and a larger back garden which the tenants were expected to keep tidy. These houses differed from their pre-war equivalents in that they were provided with an upstairs bathroom and they were more spacious.

During the 1920s S. Instone & Co were trying to increase production at Askern Colliery but the development of the pit due to the complications caused by the faulting of the coal seams was absorbing a lot of money. Nevertheless, a further 486 houses were constructed in the late 1920s and early 1930s, this time as semi-detached houses and Alfred Road, Theodore Road, Llewellyn Crescent, Davis Road, Airstone Road, Green Lane and Manor Way were laid out. Some of the streets were named after people connected with the colliery, for example Alfred and Theodore were Samuel Instone's brothers, Mr Llewellyn-Jones was the pit manager and Mr Davis and Mr Airstone were directors of the colliery company.

Instone Terrace was built in the early 1920s. These houses were considerably larger than their pre First World War counterparts in the older part of Instoneville in that they were equipped with upstairs bathrooms and front and rear gardens which the tenants were expected to keep in good order. (Postcard by James Simonton & Sons, Balby, Doncaster).

Above: Lady Alice Instone and Sir Samuel Instone pictured on 31st May 1930 at the opening of the Miners Welfare Park in Askern. They are shown surrounded by eager youngsters who no doubt later that day enjoyed the playing equipment. (Stan Longley Collection). *Below:* Postcard by James Simonton c1932 showing a queue of children for the slide at the Children's Corner in the Miners Welfare Park.

By the end of the decade the Askern Garden City Utility Association had built 662 houses which, when added to the 255 built by the Askern Estates Co. before the First World War, brought the total number of houses owned by the colliery company to 917, a figure which was still considerably shorter than the 2,366 houses that had been proposed back in 1911.

In the 1920s The Doncaster Mutual Co-operative Society opened a second Askern branch on Sutton Road and the West Riding County Council opened Selby Road and Moss Road schools to serve the increasing population. In 1923 the Askern Hotel was opened in the fork between Doncaster and Sutton Roads by Mappin's Masborough Old Brewery of Rotherham and in 1924 the Spa Hydropathic Institute was converted into the Miners Welfare Institute to serve the social needs of the workforce.

On 31st May 1930 the Miners Welfare Park was opened by Sir Samuel Instone and Lady Alice Instone on a site between Sutton Road and Doncaster Road. The Park featured tennis courts, bowling greens, football and cricket pitches as well as a playground for children. In the 1960s when the Spa Hydro building was demolished the Miners Welfare moved to new purpose built premises adjacent to the Miners Welfare Park.

Following nationalisation of the coal industry the houses of Instoneville passed into the ownership of the N.C.B. who overnight became the biggest landlord in the country. The 1950s & 1960s saw another influx of population into the area when miners from the coalfields of Scotland and the North East (where their own collieries were facing closure) moved to the productive South Yorkshire coalfield. Although a few additional houses were provided at the top end of Instoneville, the majority of families moving to Askern Colliery were housed in N.C.B. and Doncaster Rural Council estates built to the north of the old village of Campsall. Some of the estates were built in the parkland of Campsall Hall after the Bacon-Frank family had vacated the area.

In the 1970s the N.C.B. embarked on a policy of reducing their housing stock and the ownership of Instoneville passed to Doncaster Metropolitan Borough Council. Subsequently many people have bought their houses from the council and Instoneville and the Campsall estates are now largely in the hands of private owners.

The old village of Askern rapidly developed into a small shopping centre to serve the needs of the new population on the doorstep. **Above:** High Street looking towards Doncaster in 1914 with well known shops Stubbs Brothers on the left and Benett's the Butchers on the right. Most of these properties have since been demolished (Walter Roelich Postcard). **Below:** High Street & Market Place about 10 years later showing the Askern Picture House, (Edgar Scrivens Postcard).

Opposite Page: Askern Colliery in the 1980s, with the 1911 date stone from the demolished No. 1 winding engine house positioned in front of the No. 2 winding engine house, together with a pair of winding wheels which formed the entrance to the site from Campsall Road. Compare this with the illustration on Page 11 showing the same building under construction. (Pat O'Grady, courtesy of www.freewebs.com/yorkshiremain).

The Manor Baths was one of five Bath Houses that surrounded Askern Lake, as depicted on this postcard by an anonymous photographer from c1905. Since the closure of Askern Colliery several local community groups are looking at promoting the Askern area and these include Askern Town Council, North Doncaster Rural Trust and Friends of Askern Lake who proudly opened a replacement ornamental bridge over the outflow from the lake in 2009.

Glossary

Barnsley Coal Seam
A seam of coal up to 10 feet thick within the Coal Measures of South Yorkshire which is only found at the surface near the town of Barnsley.

Bunker
A large container used for the storage of coal before the coal can be treated in the screens and washery of a coal preparation plant.

Cage
Steel structure used to transport men or coal filled tubs up and down the shafts. Some cages had two decks. The cage was attached by a steel rope to the winding engine.

Coal Measures
A thick sequence of rocks and strata which consists of sandstones, shales, clays and coal seams. The coal measures of Yorkshire contain around 30 different coal seams.

Coal Preparation Plant.
A building where the treatment of coal is undertaken prior to dispatch, usually containing screens, washery and a conveyor leading to a rapid loading bunker.

Coalfield (Exposed & Concealed)
An area of land above coal measure rocks. A coalfield may be "exposed", i.e. the coal measures are found at the surface, or "concealed" where they are hidden at greater depths beneath younger rocks. Doncaster is situated on a concealed coalfield where the coal measures are buried beneath Magnesian Limestone and Bunter Sandstones.

Drift
A sloping tunnel connecting coal seams to the base of the shafts or to the surface.

Fault
A geological fracture resulting from the upward or downward movement of the strata on either side.

Gob
The area left following removal of a coal seam. It is supported with waste material or allowed to collapse in a controlled way.

Headgear
A structure of wooden, steel lattice or reinforced concrete construction, situated above the shafts and used to support the winding wheel.

Longwall Mining
A method of coal working in which coal is mined from a long coal face. The coal face connects two tunnels which lead back to the base of the shafts. The coalface thus advances away from the shafts leaving an area of gob behind. This method was later replaced by retreat mining.

Main
A suffix used mainly in South Yorkshire to denote those collieries which mined the largest or main seam from the coal measures, i.e. the Barnsley Seam

Pillar and Stall Mining
A method of coal working where coal was extracted from areas known as stalls leaving pillars of coal to support the surface. Largely replaced with longwall mining due to the advance in technology in the 19th Century.

Pit
A local term for a coal mine or colliery

Rapid Loading Bunker
A large bunker containing many tons of coal which is dropped into railway wagons passing beneath the structure.

Retreat Mining
The most economical method in mining in which roadways are driven out to the extremity of the royalty to where a coal face can then be worked back towards the shaft bottom. Largely superseded longwall mining in the 1950s/1960s.

Roadways
Underground tunnels leading from the bottom of the shaft to the coal faces.

Royalty
An area of land beneath which coal can be extracted by paying a fee or royalty on every ton produced to the landowner.

Screens
A building containing numerous devices for sorting individual lumps of coal by size or weight

Shafts
A vertical tunnel from the surface to the coal seam through which the coal is extracted and men and materials can access the workings. Following a mining disaster at Hartley Colliery in Durham each colliery was required to have two shafts, downcast and upcast, to aid escape in the event of an accident. Air was pumped through the downcast shaft to ventilate the workings and then drawn out of the colliery via the upcast shaft.

Shaft Pillar
A large area of coal left intact in order to support the colliery's surface buildings and thus protect them from the effects of subsidence. Some coal was removed from the shaft pillar to form roadways or tunnels to access the underground workings.

Sinking
The process of tunnelling vertically downwards from the surface to the coal seam in order to construct a shaft, usually undertaken by workers called sinkers who specialised in this highly skilled but dangerous work.

Skip Winding
A method of winding coal up a shaft by the use of a large capacity metal container or skip. A more economical way of transport than that previously used when individual coal filled tubs were brought to the surface in a cage.

Tubbing
A waterproof casing, usually of iron, inserted into a shaft as it was sunk in order to keep back water and soft sediments.

Tubs
Small wagons used to transport coal underground.

Washery
A surface plant for dealing with the cleaning and washing of coal

Winding Engine
Engine, initially steam driven but later powered by electricity, used to raise the cages up and down the shafts.

Bibliography

Barnett, A L (1984). *The Railways of the South Yorkshire Coalfield from 1880.* RCTS Publishing, Devon.

Coalite 75th anniversary brochure (1992). Privately published by Anglo United / Coalite Smokeless Fuels, Bolsover.

Colliery Guardian (1927). *The Colliery Year Book & Coal Trades Directory.* Louis Cassier Publishing, London.

Gould S & Ayris I (1995). *Colliery Landscapes. An aerial survey of the deep-mined coal industry in England.* English Heritage / Billington Press Ltd, London.

Hill, Alan (2001). *The South Yorkshire Coalfield, a history and development.* Tempus Publishing, Stroud.

Longley, Stan (1982). *Askern Spa, a photograph album.* Waterdale Press / Doncaster Library Service.

Longley, Stan (1995). *Askern Spa, a photograph album: A further collection.* Waterdale Press / Doncaster Library Service.

Longley Stan. *Askern Colliery, Askern Coalite.* Personal albums of photographs, notes and newspaper clippings collected by Mr Longley.

Roe, Sid (2004). *A history of Askern Colliery.* BarnSCAN Local History Publications.

Thornes, Robin (1994). *Images of Industry: Coal.* Royal Commission on the historical monuments of England, Swindon.